# The Present Moment of Happiness

Jenneth Graser

*with foreword by Christine Sine
and introduction by Ana Lisa de Jong*

© 2019 Jenneth Graser

Cover Design – Jenneth Graser
(Public Domain Botanical Illustration from Biodiversity Heritage Library)

First edition – January 2019

ISBN-10: 1793380775
ISBN-13: 978-1793380777

www.secretplacedevotion.weebly.com

# endorsements

"*The Present Moment of Happiness* is a personal journey in which the poetic voice is a guiding spirit lending direction to discovery of the Divine within."

—Jamie K. Reaser, author of *Coming Home: Learning to Actively Love this World*

"Rediscover "jasmine .../ a flush of white stars flung into the kitchen." Daydream a little. Hope again. Simultaneously grounded in Creation "where moss lingers/ on the fringes of time" yet "in tune with all wings," Jenneth Graser's prayerful poems resonate: invitational, intimate as unnamed yearning, instructive as proverbs. All speak of, and with, Love, venturing among "words . . . threaded into the/ quilt of lives," where "We are all neighbors.""

—Laurie Klein, author of *Where the Sky Opens*

"*The Present Moment of Happiness* is more than a collection of poems. It is a gentle invitation to explore our relationship with God, more bravely than before. Jenneth paints a sacred space with her words and the ordinary soon becomes the extraordinary. These are words born from personal struggle, that draw one in to listen to His tender voice that speaks healing over our brokenness. They are a beautiful reminder to seek the sacred in the mundane and for us to be expectant for more of Him, despite the hardship of our journey."

—Liezel Graham, *www.liezelgraham.com*

"Jenneth Graser's book, *The Present Moment of Happiness* is a reflective gift of poetry where the writer's heart/soul are open and revealing to writing her personal journey with God. Honest, vulnerable and accepting as to how Spirit moves through her in her beautiful writing we hear healing threads of honesty, listening, and renewing through these pages and periods of her life. Jenneth's mystical voice teaches and sings at the same time. She guides one through moment after moment of experiences in nature, relationship and specifically with the God who is in our present moments, bringing revelation and deep contentment."

—Donna Knutson, author of *Finding God on Mayberry Street: Seasons of Spirituality in Poems and Reflections*

"*The Present Moment of Happiness* is a rare jewel - literary poetry about one's love story with The Trinity God. These poems have no clichés, are not didactic, and are raw full of lines that give that poetic punch right in the heart. Each of the senses are experienced in these poems: the scent of an orange in "The Present Moment of Happiness:" the touch of His hand in "The Beautiful Man;" the sound of the river in "A Tree Psalm;" watching the rain in "When the Day Was Set to Unravel, Here You Are;" the speaking of weeping in "Tiny Seeds;" and the tasting of stars in "You Will Find Your Flight.""

—Chris Rice Cooper, *https://chrisricecooper.blogspot.com*

"Jenneth Graser's poems in "The Present Moment of Happiness" gift us with all the paradox of true poetry: a feast for the senses, and also a pathway beyond the senses, emotional richness and also the peace beyond the peaks and valleys of our emotional lives. Reading her work, our humanity is fed with the magic of ordinary experience, and our connection to divinity is gently, deeply opened. Inside, between, around the words: love. The residue of reading her work: happiness and love."

—Brooke McNamara, author of *Feed Your Vow, Poems for Falling into Fullness*

*Dedication*

I dedicate this book, born out of a season of recovery and letting go, to my dear family without whose support this would not have been possible. To my Precious Husband Karl, who believes in me through thick and thin, always encouraging me to pursue my dreams and who is a tremendous example to me, a man of courageous generosity. And to my dear daughters, Abigail, Sophia and Joelle, who have shaped my life in countless ways and whose love and support of me shine brightly in my life every day. I love and appreciate you with all my heart and dedicate this book to each one of you.

# Foreward

I have never met Jenneth Graser. I live half a world away from her, yet I find that her poetry reaches out across the miles to touch my soul. Like Jenneth I have discovered the beauty and the joy of translating my thoughts and emotions into written prayers and poems. Like her I have found that the writing of such prayers and poems helps me to slow down, breathe deeply and take notice of the voice of God bubbling up from deep within me. Much to my surprise I find that poetry like this is a powerful force that can transform not only my own life but also the lives of others who read them and allow them to resonate in their hearts.

Both the writing of poetry and the reading of poems are experiences that stir all our senses in a profound way. It is not just about words. Sometimes we begin with a word. At other times it is a thought or an image that resonates in our minds. It calls to us, perhaps out of the depths of our pain, or through flashes of intense joy and awe inspiring wonder. The image grows and takes shape emerging into words that burst out of our mouths. We recite them aloud, sensing the vibrations not just in our ears but also in our hearts and minds. They pluck at our heartstrings and slowly we craft them into a cascade of verses that brings healing and refreshment in mind, soul and body.

The Bible is full of poetic images like this that pull at our heartstrings and beckon us to listen to the voice of God, healing and cleansing our spirits on the way. Yet sometimes we feel that these ancient books cannot fully express what is bubbling up within us. Spoken prayers and words of adoration and praise don't seem to do it either. We need the language of modern poetry that enables us to interpret the pain and the joy of life in our own unique and expressive way.

There are a number of reasons why poetry is particularly suited to the expressing of our emotions. First, emotional undertones are hard to put into words. Metaphor and imagery often help us give voice to them. Second, the use of rhythm taps into powerful nonverbal responses, in much the same way that music does. Even the abstract nature of poetry is a powerful tool that makes it easier to take a closer look at painful experiences which can be threatening to us if we try to approach them in a direct manner.

My prayer poems are an integral part of my daily devotions. I have written many of them on cards with one of my photos in the background. I carry them with me as I travel and pull them out throughout the day to refocus my world on God. Some have become canvas prints that sit on my prayer altar and provide a focus each morning for my thoughts and worship of God. This practice has greatly enriched my life and drawn me closer to God in special and unexpected ways.

My prayer is that these poems that Jenneth has gathered will stir your hearts and souls too. I hope they will not just draw you closer to God but stir you to craft your own prayers and poems that help you express your life experiences in profound new ways.

> May your heart beat to the rhythm of eternal breath,
> Your spirit be filled with the wonder of eternal presence,
> Your life embrace the joy of eternal love.
> May you know the Eternal One,
> In you, around you, before you, behind you.
> May you welcome the Triune God
> In every thought and word and deed.

Christine Sine - contemplative activist, author and facilitator of godspace-light.com

# Introduction

It gives me great delight to write the Introduction to my friend Jenneth Graser's book *The Present Moment of Happiness*. For those who have not yet met Jenneth in your journeying, or been blessed to partake of her bountiful words, I feel excited for you and the discoveries you are yet to make, and the ways in which Jenneth's words will touch you personally.

Jenneth's poetry, is an unmasking. At first we might find ourselves feeling slightly vulnerable, as she holds up a mirror with her words to our naked humanity, our common yet unique emotions, inadequacies, challenges, longings and losses. It can be unnerving for a moment to feel such vulnerability, to receive the invitation Jenneth gives out to us, with exquisite tenderness, but soon we start to breathe, feel our hearts swell up into the space her words create in us, and in which we continue to expand as we gift ourselves self-acceptance and compassion in response. And our souls open that bit more to the light, our strength returns and healing begins, and the dreams, and true selves we had folded and put away in a drawer, we shake and hang out again in the sun, welcoming them as re-united friends.

As I sit and write this I am re-reading Jenneth's powerful words and reflecting on the New Zealand Native Kowhai tree in flower outside my window, the blooms for which I wait with bated breath each spring. For much of the year I pass the Kowhai tree by, in that spot where it keeps its sacred place in the garden, quietly standing and bearing all its energies on preparation for its annual unveiling. At which time its bright yellow flowers emerge one by one, and then in overwhelming abundance, and the waiting birdlife, in particular the beautiful New Zealand Tui, ascend upon it to devour its sweetness and spread its goodness.

In such a way Jenneth's poetry creeps up upon us. Her elegant phrases stand alone, and together with dignity and power, and we respond with appreciation and admiration, and then all of a sudden, as though an avalanche of blossom were poured upon us, we feel a bit overcome, a bit undone by truth and beauty, and we find ourselves, like new-born babes at the breast, feeding from a generous abundance, a harvest of fruit to feed the hungry heart. And these words, open us to our own words, speak to us inwardly, as we feed upon them, until in time, as Jenneth notes in her poetry, we start to 'relinquish the words for the meaning'. And we find ourselves standing at our place in time, feeling that little bit braver and stronger, that little bit healed, under a heavenly flowering.

Jenneth describes this much awaited volume of poetry as being reflections out of a time of brokenness, and healing. She describes it as being 'broken into wonder'. I can see through her words, my dear friend Jenneth growing from loss, like a thirsty tree deepening its roots at the river bank and drawing sustenance from the living waters. In the re-assembling of herself and the recasting of her dreams, we see how she has become the self which God has perhaps always envisaged her as being, but as Jenneth says 'we never stop growing into eternity'. May I add, in the meantime, we shed ourselves as gifts for others.

As Jenneth herself says,

'I am a flower falling on the stream,

and floating in spirals of letting go,

as my dreams make way for you'.


Ana Lisa de Jong - Living Tree Poetry

Author of the *Poetry for the Soul* series and *Songs of the Heart*. A two volume set, comprised of the books *Heart Psalms* and *Thrice Blessed*.

D ear Reader, I invite you into this collection of poems for your times of contemplation.

Poetry and prayer are for me interchangeable ways to relate with God. These poems are for slowing down into a spacious interior place where God is alive and moving within.

The rapid pace of life with an often constant buzz of technology and pressure can lead to feelings of stress as we try to keep up. Time with God can sometimes feel like a luxury, when it is in fact our life-source.

This collection of free verse comes mainly from my blog *Prayers on the Wing* and has been written out of a transitional time. It is an exploration of what it is to be with God in places of healing and of being broken into wonder.

I encourage you to read each poem once through, and then read it again until something stands out to you. Take this and listen for deeper insight to come. Allow time to breathe softly into the revelation you receive.

You are a pilgrim on a journey into your listening heart. When you come to God with your yes, anything becomes possible.

With love and blessings,

Jenneth

# Live In The Moment

Every breath is happening now.

When you become aware

of your heart beating,

the present moment

unfolds as a gift.

Ease into the present

and feel all of time blossom.

It has been here all along,

just waiting to be discovered.

Jenneth Graser

## The Present Moment of Happiness

Peeling this orange with the best peeler
I've ever had, the zest tickles my nostrils
and sends citrus endorphins dancing
through my brain.

One moment to remember
like déjà vu, what it is to be
present and forsake all things.

Heaven opens up like a jigsaw puzzle
and explains nothing to me:
not why I have been born
for such a time as this, not
what my future may be,

But my thoughts take a javelin leap
over the mandarin moment
into the furthest reaches of
the galaxies, beyond time and
definitions of eternity in math
books for the professionals.

And a hand is laid upon my
shoulder that I cannot see,
and spins me like a merry-go-round
of blurry children in the park,
and I'm drawn to one revelation:

The sounds I hear, the things I see,
the breath I breathe, the taste,
the taste of this orange bursting
into each individual juicy follicle
of happiness.

## The Beautiful Man

There is a bench
in a garden, weathered,
the wood worn,
knots coiled where moss lingers
on the fringes of time.

Here she sits side by side
with the Beautiful Man.

He has taken her hand
where no words are spoken.

The walls around the garden
do not withhold from her
a single thing.

There is growth perpetual where
conversation has folded
between the palms of their hands.

She comes here to brew in stillness,
to feel the rush immaterial fade,
to merge with what is eternal -

To feel the flavours between them
infuse.

Jenneth Graser

## A Tree Psalm

I am a tree deepening my roots
into the earth.

Every word of your Spirit is encircling my heart
with each ring in the trunk of the passing of years,
making your word a part of me.

I am a tree beside the river
flowing under my leaves.

I listen for the wisdom that daily comes
on the breath of your Spirit
and meditate day and night
on the wisdom you give.

I am a tree delighting in life
with the sun through my leaves.

I am a green cathedral of stained-glass
windows of healing leaves and
fruit that comes in season.

I am a tree that grows without striving
as a tree must grow,
and I lift my branches every day to Heaven
and I worship the One who made me.

Every day my roots delve deeper.

## Halfway to the Other Side

We have shifted sideways
where shadows lengthen the lawn
and we have parted with grieving.

The pathways through the garden
have been to us a maze of high hedges
manicured to perfection and yet,
too high to see over.

A cul-de-sac appears around every corner
and we have persevered so as to navigate
ourselves into other dead-ends.

A hole in the hedge reveals
a window through which to peer
and there is the house we have been
searching for.

A river runs under the house
and cools the feet after so long a walk.
Every room is lined with books
where words are threaded into the
quilt of lives lived halfway to the other side.

The trees still speak to us, as always.
But we have asked the gardener to kindly
open more doorways for us.
He told me, they have been there all along.

## Resting Seat

There are many things that could be said,
many that could be done.

Mountains to climb, up to the very top,
lists of the bucket kind.

A feeling of to-do lingers at the fringes of the day
as we drop exhausted into bed.

And Lord you are calling us,
you are calling us still...

*Come my Beloved,*
*into a time outside of time.*

*Come to the resting seat in the garden*
*of my habitation.*

There are no nagging voices or things to be done.

*Here, there is presence that guides*
*everything you do on earth.*

Listen to my voice, put on the music, lay aside your rushing.

*Move into the pace of ease where my Spirit speaks*
*strength into your frame.*

*And whatever you need to face,*
*we will face it together.*

## When the Day Was Set to Unravel, Here You Are

The steam from the cup of tea
has become a ministry of your presence.

When the day was set to unravel, here you are.

Rain collects across the valley in sheets
and from my window I watch it come
into the garden from afar, blown in from the sea.

The expanse of your heart is infinitely large
in every breath waiting to be realised.

If it cannot be in the things I have wanted,
then it can be in what's in front of my eyes
waiting to be seen.

Awareness is: becoming a part
of the miracles in the moment I am living.

Belonging in your love, opens me
to the beautiful genius of your creation
in a humble beetle folded in with the washing
crawling free.

Or a moth on the curtain, fuzzy creeping over
my fingers onto the windowsill.

I am grateful for the things that don't always
work the way I want them to.

They are teaching me into patience,
a patience that has not always been so forthcoming.

If I stop wanting so badly,
I will dip deeply into this moment and draw forth
an infinity of living waters.

## Relinquish the Words

You may be walking into a forest
and smelling everything -
the cones crushed underfoot,
the sap rising.

You may be navigating stones
on the shore of countless waves.

You may be learning to re-love
your own heart again
and making time for a line of birds
on the mid-point of the horizon.

You may be wondering whatever
happened to the grace of first wonder?

You may be checking yourself
for holes in your pockets.

But your body is surrounded by trees and water,
your mind is bowing down
and your spirit is in tune with all wings.

You may be wondering what you are doing
here after all these years?

You may be pausing to observe the hour.

Waves thrust your toes deep into sand
and you stumble upon the sky speaking
your language.

You are being birthed upon yourself
and learning to relinquish the words
for the meaning,

while feathers drift out of the sun
and settle at your feet.

## Move into Prayer

You filled a space in your diary
for a date with yourself today.

You switch off your phone.
No demands on your attention.

You decide to walk down to the park -
you know of a place not many go.

A glade of trees among trees
and leaves in a state of holy ebb,
where a stream flows beneath it all.

Into the peace, you quietly tread.
Every voice silenced, one by one.

Each thought sighs into the ground
as a seed on your breath.

Your hands are ladles
for water scooped from a river
that quenches, a parched mind.

This is your cathedral -
worship, a humble song
under the cavern of green light

You move into prayer.

## Meet Me in Slow Time

Decelerate our moments
Meet me in slow time
Plunge me into grace.

Stop the clock,
Suspend reality...

Meet me in paints and song
Sing with me in oil pastel,
Drift with the tide.

Brush stroke me into being
Deep determined impressions
Of light, of dark,

Of coming into ourselves
Outside of time.

## We Have Found a Good Home

Our hands lay palms upon knees
and we have rested.

Breath upon breath
and we have listened.

Hope leads to greater hope
and we have moved quietly.

It all comes to us gradually
that we belong.

We have searched
until we realise we are found.

We knock
and the door opens wide.

We have stopped looking
for meaning elsewhere.

We have found a good home
here.

# Hope

When circumstances get you down,

it takes courage to allow hope

to grow within.

There is an invitation to receive hope

and welcome it,

even when it feels like a morsel

is all you have.

A morsel of courage added to hope

will cause it to expand.

As hope expands, your vision will too.

## A Pilgrim in Your Arms

I am beyond the mountain now
No more round and round for me.
Lord, it was too alluring to think
I could get somewhere by going nowhere.

I stepped away from the same old same old
And found myself a pilgrim in your arms.

People have become strangers of grace
Born into flesh with eyes mounted in souls
Looking into my eyes,
And greeting us silently.

I have a palm in front of me, holding nothing but hope.
I have a palm beside me, holding nothing but your hand.

Lord you are wise beyond your years,
I know your laugh from deep within
Is an earthquake to my old ways of doing and thinking.
And as the ground of my yesterlife crackcrumbles around me

I am finding your heart is a field with no fences.
I am looking and seeing with my deeper eyes.
I am hearing your voice packaged in many voices
All singing.

Jenneth Graser

## What Hurts and What Is Healing

I find myself open to sound,
Quiet on the morning's gift.

Dancing waves of Arabic rhythm
Syncopate with the formation of
Every letter on the page.

There is forgiveness to be released.
Myself reminded, our own treasures
Grow in the blessings we bestow, unmerited.

People wait today
For art to dip into their pain with something
To show how grateful adoration
Appeases loss.

People waiting as a gift between the
Holding walls of my abode.

The gift I capture with my hands
Open wide in thanks, to let each soar away
And settle on my shoulder
Of their own free choice.

I find myself a radiant blessing on the eye's
Reflection of the man who loves me so;
He does not need reminding that his bliss is mine
And mine is to be his, always.

I find myself open, and opening wider.
I find myself new and old, both new and old.

I find myself placed, inside the place
That feels just right for me to be for
Now, alongside what hurts and is healing,

Both: what hurts and what is healing.

## Wait for Resurrection

Leave every watch and clock behind.
Go to places the earth receives
the barefooted pleasure of you.

Where you are able to
notice yourself as a breathing,
living human being.

Emotions may rise and fall
with the spending of a day
on what seems like nothing.

But there are tears here
that come on laughter and on pain.

And there are tears of another kind
when beside the tomb of evil fruits,
you walk straight into a man weeping.

Interpretations of reality
are determined by your
outlook on life accumulated.

But sit with God
from the viewpoint of things eternal
and you realise love must still be greater.

Awareness steeped
in veins of blood that ran
for all mankind,
transforms our ability to
really see.

We are changed by the tears God sheds
at the mouth of every tomb that
waits for resurrection.

## Dark Place of Trust

Gideon managed really well
when he needed sure confirmation.

There were undeniable miracles.

Even so, his heart must have
trembled on the first, yes God
I will.

We want a sign:
audible voice from the heavens,
word of knowledge,
and a wonder:
dove to alight on our shoulder
with a message sent.

A fleece will also do.
To prove that what we feel
is really what you are asking of us.

But Thomas reached in on the wounds
in your side with the words:
Blessed are those who do not see
and yet believe.

So are we blessed then,
when we forgo the need for signs
and enter more deeply into the dark
place of trust?

It is love that has been waiting
there for us
in our falling.

## What It Is to Be Seen

It is not a simple matter of arriving,
but of listening into the times we have been given.

We have scrambled for truth between the lines
and those who have aged through selfless acts of kindness
are hidden in the cracks of the world.

It is all in the eyes, he said.
The eyes we have dared to face with our eyes,
until we know what it is to be seen.

Seen with the fire that blazed the suns into being
and the love that causes knees to fold
and the power that causes rocks to weep

and we have felt the tears well up from
within the places no words are spoken

and the spirit has a voice most clear

and all of the things that have fallen down
or away, pale before these ruptures of light,

because we are made from such love, to be loved.
Yes, we are made from such love, to be love.

## I Come

Down the steps I come
Dry, thirsty I come, parched
I come.

I step into the water
My feet in the well
My legs in the well
My hands, heart, soul
My head, mind, spirit
In the well.

I drink.
I bathe.
I float in the water
I drift.

I look at the sky
The birds, clouds
Sky.

I will be ready to
Do your will once again
When the dryness of me
Is taken by your quench.
Until then,
I come.

## Inner Landscape

My mountain of heart valleys into deep red,
It climbs heights into flush of dawn.

I ascend into my brain, view the territory, right and left
Rivers of thought, pathways of hope, doubt, dreams, fears.

I bungee jump into my chest and listen to my lungs
Expand, contract expand, each breath a gift.

It is time to pioneer the unknown terrain
Of the soul of my innermost parts.

I will dig into my spirit to search for secret treasure.
The deep will fill with my seeking eyes.

I will find the scroll of promises kept for me
And dance in the night to music composed for such a moment.

Jenneth Graser

## You wait for me on the other side

Where do you lift the dawn from her slumber,
turn back the sheets of the night
as showers of rain catch the morning's yearning?

Where do you bury the days long gone?
The hands that reach for the next moment
are bones now at rest under the shore.

How do you hold a new born baby?
When she took so long to come and flesh of your flesh
now rests at your breast and suckles there, my baby oh.

How do you seal the perfect moment?
Play, repeat, and play again:
The turn of your face in the angles of evening
when the sun presses down on the soul.

What became of the music we played
when we walked through the door?
It circled our feet, and flew up
with the clanging of the bells.

I don't yet know what your face looks like, when
we've been walking blind in two dimensions
closer than skin folds.

On the threshold of the spirit
You wait for me on the other side.

I hear my singing in the night hours –
all the windows thrown into the wind
as the clouds rush by.

## It Is Not So Hard to Go Within After All

It is not so hard to go within after all.

Open the gate of my garden home,
breathe on top of the morning chill, a song.

I feel you urge me towards the sanctuary.

It is more thorough than before,
when I was so busy searching for what is lost.

The windows frame what is so familiar
and yet, it's all become a platform of the spectacular.

The shadows on the curtain were not there before
and now they are pulsing on the fabric cascade.

The jasmine that was closed in bud
is now a flush of white stars flung into the kitchen.

I was looking to move on, feel different,
get on with mid-life into whatever's next
and now I've been surprised into your face.

I've come to the grass under the knee,
I've come to the flowers in the grass
and all that lives under the grass.

I've come to the smallness of life
where your largeness is hidden.

Your face is growing with the roots
quietly interlaced and drinking
all the earth has to offer.

## Adrift

On the cusp of the already
and the not as yet,
I am carried on gossamer silken
threads.

High into the thermals, seeds
made for being carried on winds
rise in circular navigation
and I go with it.

I feel gravitation as a memory
and thought as a possible stance,
but Spirit knows what is best
and so I acquiesce.

It has been a tremor
of fluctuating postulations
without getting to grips
with any formula.

A mystery must remain so
until, leaps across time
make conjunctions with reason.

Perhaps a year will take me
to the root of the great oak;
for now I am carried, hushed
across treetops.

For now I am touching base
with the uppermost leaves
at the soles of my feet
and drifting higher.

Then higher again.

# Love Yourself

Sometimes life goes by

at such a frenzied pace,

you end up putting yourself last

on the agenda.

It is time to get to really know yourself

with unconditional love.

When you embrace yourself as a true friend,

love overflows into everything else.

Generously loving yourself

will energise your whole life.

Jenneth Graser

## Lord, Let Me Receive Myself with Love

Lord, let me receive myself with love.

I walk towards myself,

As though I face me, in the lounge.
There I sit by the fire,
With creasethebrow thoughts on my mind.

I sit down, beside myself,
I hold my hands as my surprised face looks up,
To see me there.

I will look into my eyes
Into the hidden dark and hidden light

Then, I will embrace myself.

I will receive myself with love.

## Tiny Seeds

He moistened the hem of her robe,
led her by both hands.

The green of the forest was under her feet,
now there is only water.

The fire ate up most of the mountains,
with a sound of seeds popping.

She used excuses by the dozen, offered
to herself and to others.

By late October, tendrils appeared
and her fears were dealt with in dreams.

Ecclesiastes called for seasons of planting,
with a time to weep and a time to laugh.

The grass had a chance once again, as
blackened earth and charred roots gave way.

The soles of her feet were too used to stones.
She came alone from the desert to the trees calling.

Her tiny seeds have sprouted
in the hands of her Lover.

## Marvellous Things

Learn to travel within the
present moments of time
before you phone a travel agent.

Mark off significant realms -
do your research well.

Be comfortable with
unknown unmapped places.

You may travel the inner places
with peace and no judgement.

Explore beyond what you know.

You can be OK with heading
for shores dangerous.

You can be generous towards
yourself, and let the dust settle,
be blown away.

God has been known to shape
marvellous things out of dust.

## You Will Find Your Flight

A double transition occurs
when your outward journey
mirrors the journey of your heart.

Outward change does not
clamour so, when inward
resolution has been made.

Forgive well, travel memory
with tenderness.

Map out newly explored terrain
in such a way
that other pilgrims may benefit.

Observe the larger hand of grace
at work.

The heart of a traveller is called
to find rest within,
so that restless urges do not drive
the motion.

Travel deep, dear Pilgrim,
find the peace you are searching for.

Travel high, dear Pilgrim,
taste the stars and drink the rain.

There is so much ahead.
You won't be driven.
You will be deeply moved.

You will find your flight.

Jenneth Graser

## I Shall Not Want

I walk the path between trees
down into the glade
and place my soul into the water there.

A river alive with stones
awash with every story of my life
flowing downwards to the sea.

I am a flower falling on the stream
and floating in spirals of letting go
as my dreams make way for you.

I am my truest self in the song David sings,
each word unveils the longing of my heart:
*I shall not want.*

## Rest in the Centre of Things

Under the river, the riverbed
Under the mountain, cavernous rooms.
Under my mind, my heart rests.

Beneath the roots, the water
Under the waterfall, the pool so deep.
Under the sea, great darkness in crevices.

Under my mind, my mouth, my speech
Observations of word and thought.
Under the boat, a rudder.

Beneath the hen, chicks are warmed
Under the feathers, the skin.
Below the clouds, the rain falls.

Beneath the surface of appearance
The reality abides -
Underneath the symptoms, the source.

Under the heart, the Godhead hides
At rest in the centre of things.

At rest in the centre of things.

## Hidden

It is good to be hidden in the great garden.
It is good to be hidden in rain.

It is good to be under the fingerprints
of green foliage among trees.

It is good to be hidden in the hand, in prayer,
to be under the wing.

To be hidden by wave upon wave, and behind the waterfall.

To be hidden in the womb and the fluff of the nest,
to be held in the cloth of motherly care.

To be under the night sky of a new moon
in the middle of a field looking into star upon star,
in the grass, hidden.

Such times were given to us so that we may listen,
and speak and be heard.

So that we may find ourselves
alone in the presence of greatness.

So that we may know we
are small

and yet find the universe is expanding on our breath
and upon each thought as we crest the tides
of love in the place of being
hidden.

## Spread-Wide Heart

Some looks speak what words have no chance to say.
It takes a willing spirit to drop the keys
and resolve to take in the pages of speech
that will pour forth expansive.

You grow yourself discerning
when you draw from wisdom
by following undefined paths
to places that welcome all seekers.

The paths that take you first low
to where water runs deep,
before you take what you have learned
and declare it from the mountains.

Be with the small insignificant
things that feel like they are going
nowhere and achieving not much.

Notice where love hides
under the bling of what looks
more outwardly appealing.

There are treasures to be found
in unexpected places.

When you have gathered the
intricate lessons contained in
humble undergrowth,
you may be trusted to give away pearls.

When giving becomes to you
more beautiful than losing or gaining,
the immaculate compassion of
your spread-wide heart will take in
more than enough of goodness,
you won't have room for it.

Spilling goodness abundant
from what you found in tiny obscure places,
when you noticed that eternity
was buried there.

## Holy Disruption

We have grown in the vine.
We have had our withered branches
cut off.

We have felt a promise of fruitfulness
surge through with juicy sap
and learned to be grateful
for the things that have fallen away.

A holy disruption
is necessary.

It is good to be disrupted:
to have our feathers ruffled,
to be shaken up a bit,
to see things in a new way.

When we are hurled into the sky,
it is then that
we will find our wings.

## We will Be Pilgrims

We traverse terrain
Cut out of the mountain
By the ones before us,
Who paid the sacrificial cost.

To harrow out a road
In the rock, with guts and sweat
Mixed with granite dust?
Trailing tears.

You may dream of another life,
But fresh perspective is only
Possible when willing
To fork off the trampled path.

We will do the pilgrim thing,
No, we will be
Pilgrims.

Keep my heart out of the stone
With the strength of Kilimanjaro
Rising.

Keep my mind out of the dirt,
But down to the earth
Rooted.

And my spirit, must be kept
Beyond all earthly things:
Keep it with your Spirit

Cumulonimbus soaring.

# Believe

Your destiny is fuelled by belief.

Every time you take a risk

to believe bravely,

God is right there to meet you.

He matures faith within,

as you nourish

and feed it with promises.

Confident faith

enlarges your heart

and keeps you poised in God's goodness.

## May We Rise

May we rise
As eagles who lean on thermals.
May we rise into the music,
Into the sky and higher.

May we rise
Above the turbulent waters of many conflicts,
Above the need to figure it all out.

May we rise above the thirsty earth,
Above the insatiable need for more
And then higher.

May we rise above the past, present, future
And breathe through timeless places.

May we rise into the great company
Of witnesses, all welcoming.

May we rise into the essence of prayer
And unconditional being.

May we rise into the fragrance of worship
Where every note creates a new possibility.

May we rise into Ascension,
May we rise in resurrection.

And there let us be taken
On the thermals of many praises
Where only higher we may find ourselves
At one with all Love is.

## New Realms of My Being

I am in the now moment with you
Loving Spirit.

I am a phoenix of fire and special tongues,
There is a surprise in every unfurling of wings.

 You are mystery and journey,
 The road of you leads ever onwards.

Spirit of my temple, I have not arrived in you,
I have begun to be birthed.

Some of me has passed away
To make space for your great furnace.

I have found the pleasure of ever unfoldingness.
The discovery of heart that grows
Large large larger in the dark and in the light.

I have found not arrival, but rather departure...
Into new realms of your Being.

Into new realms of my being
In you.

## Doing Nothing with God

Take off your sandals
and bask under the fire of God's eyes.

Enter the Sabbath rest
for the children.

There is a wonderfully blessed woman
who works into the night.

She is learning to forgo duty;
where tenderness holds idle hands.

Mary has made herself vulnerable,
casting aside all care of what the people say.

But there is a time and a season
for every activity under the face of heaven.

And she has chosen a burning bush
for now.

She would put aside all work dutiful,
to soak in the strength that comes

From doing nothing
with God.

Jenneth Graser

## The Sound of Amen

Fill my day with the sound of Amen
So be it, let it be.

Let the Amen fill my soul,
Whisper it through my mind.

The rest of it leans into your chest
At the feasting table
Breaking bread, drinking wine

I lean into your chest with the sound of it,

Amen.

## Make Room for You

It is time to make room for you
to come in ways I have not known.

My heart has become eager for the stretch
of tent pegs and widening of stakes.

The pain of a good stretch will be worth it,
to receive the mystery of your voice in the shade.

I will meet with you in places unfamiliar
and break bread with you, and drink wine.

I will linger over your features
and we will be silent for awhile.

I may not feel like talking,
you may not feel like talking too.

But we will be with the love that grows
through all things hard in a breaking of ground.

We will stay and observe what may come
from such a union, where old love feels new.

As our hearts synchronise,
we hear the rhythm combined.

## Yet, He Would Kneel for You

His vast intelligence
Called a universe into mathematical being.

Andromeda, Tucana, Triangulum, Centaurus.

Yet, he would kneel for you
With a towel wrapped around his body

To present you with a bowl.

He would take your feet, one by one,
Swirl them in warm water reflecting candlelit stars,

Wash them carefully, Spirit hovering.

Pour fresh water over them and take them
Into his towel to be dried,

To be clean.

## Your Face at My Table

We stand at the door of your knocking
and open wide
to the light of your countenance.

Come, we will sit down.

We will be together,
enfolded in peace though there
are many uncertainties at play.

This is the true
bold reality we live for;
your face at our table as yet unseen.

This is the banquet
we have waited to share with you.

Come, let us eat, let us drink.

And we will be filled,
our thirsts will be quenched,
and our hungers will rest.

## Neighbours

He took the leprous and unsightly hands
of a woman kicked to the outskirts.

He took them in his own and pressed every doubt
out of mind with one word, *Clean*.

He saw hope where there was no
rightful reason for hope to be and yet,

I will come to your house.
I will eat with you.

With a calling forth, his words
brought life where there was none.

He takes my breath into a place air is sweet
and gives me space inside my chest
to take in beauty beyond the pain of it.

My womanly being is welcomed where
perfume breaks open on moments like these.

Every soul is seen with eyes that see,
without constraints or definitions narrow.

Love has shaped every person born.
We are all neighbours.

## Angels on Their Way Somewhere

The signs of the times
point in many directions.

Many a soul has felt the
overwhelming need for a map
that would lay out the path
in such a way
that GPS would not be necessary.

We want to tap into the glory
that fills the earth
as the waters do the sea.

We want our eyes opened
like the servant of Elisha,
to realise there are more for us
than against us.

We would like to see flaming chariots
and to hear the words:
"You need only to be still,
the Lord will fight for you."

Much goes on behind the scenes,
we have no notion of.

Angels walk the streets
in the centre of much commotion
and no matter what the eye may see,
greater are those with us.
Greater too the one who resides
within us.

Our prayers do matter.
The livening presence of God works through us
into a place of first love compassion
for the world, it was always
intended for everyone.

We can see our prayers fly alongside
the angels on their way somewhere
to help someone who really needs it.

We do make a difference.

Jenneth Graser

## Pearls in the Dark

I am drawn to you looking at
Me from beyond the veil.
On wafts of incense and icon

Your instruments tell tales of
Other places, distant times,
Families.

Where to be all grown up
Looks altogether different.
On woven threads of colour,

Many feet dance as fabric swirls the air.
Prayers sigh from cliff to cliff
In flight between the mountains.

You discover God in the way
Your grandmother tells stories.
Firelight flickers a ritual between

The folds and wrinkles of her face.
You experience the presence of
God in the beating of your drum.

As you light each candle, the words
Fold from the scrolls, chanted.
All of your senses seek and discover

Pearls in the dark; you share so kindly.

# Grateful Dreaming

Some seasons bring you

to the painful surrender of dreams.

As strength is poured into weakness,

new dreams start to whisper.

Grateful thanks will overtake disappointment

when you truly realise,

God means more to you than anything else.

You place every dream into God's hands this time,

because you know your hands are too small.

When your dreams are in the care of God,

they will grow bigger than you.

## The Veil Grew Thin

Before we were born,
we were known.

And there was a day your words
filled the atmospheres with light
for the very first time.

There is always a before.

Before you were conceived
in confines of a womb,
Bright Morning Star.

You became little -
Precious Baby, God so small;
rejected from an inn to the hay
on a night the veil grew thin on hallelujahs.

God in the form of flesh contained
in a vessel of earth-bound love
for your human travels.

All of your omnipotence
given over to the brunt of nail,
body against wood and thrusting sword.

For our smallness to be lifted in
the fullness of infinite grace,
and so, to live forever.

## Misfits

Collect your tears from the face of the sky,
Clouds do not refrain.

Be with the dew suspended on the leaf,
Drip into the river waiting.

Sigh on the highest mountain breeze
Where it is difficult to breathe.

Open a gift with fingers tentative,
As though it is the only gift you may receive.

Grateful thanks may rise with greater thanks
When borne through the ashes.

Be with roots who remember the music of light.
In dark places, go deeper.

Live with an egg in its stages,
On a nest of what is to come.

Be with composting fruit on the manure pile;
A steam of matter rises from loss.

Once you were content to smile at flowers -
Now you bury your nose into scent.

Once you were happy to watch from airport windows -
Now you have booked your flight.

Other travellers have made room for your beauty,
Misfits have joined hands in strange peace.

## The Layers of Thanksgiving

Open the day with thanks
as you shrug back the curtains into the view.
Stop for a moment, remain.

Peel back the layers of thanksgiving:

1. everything beautiful in your past to be grateful for.

Delve deeper and you find:

2. the painful things that have shaped your life for good.

Go into a new layer and you find:

3. the small, seemingly insignificant things that make a difference.

Deeper again, peel off another layer:

4. gratitude for the present moment.

Then you become thankful for:

5. the patience you learn through irritations.

6. the challenging people who teach you to love and forgive.

7. the big things you often take for granted.

Then you discover thanks for:

8. the best that is yet to come.

The emotion of gratitude takes over
and you realise the layers won't ever stop,
because at the ever-unveiling heart of thanksgiving you find,
something invaluable:

9. the spirit of contentment.

## Dare to Shine

You have felt for some time the pull
of simplicity.

A lowering of certain expectations
to make room for what comes.

The peeling of a shroud
of weighty obligation,
to step out like a newborn.

Switch off the lying voices loud.
Dial up on a whisper of promises.

Look at your self in the mirror.
Remove the labels they put there.

You can rearrange the territory
and prepare for what did not feel so safe before.

Take off the mask to let your skin
breathe in the fair light of day.
Reach out for help when help is needed.

No more running for cover -
You will dare to shine.

## Dream Dancer

She has taken off the clothes
of borrowed dreams
and stepped into the wardrobe
of colour, texture, drop and line.

Gingerly, she reaches out
for gloves of new purpose
and dares to linger over
jewels, plentiful.

It is time to slip into
delicate intention,
to feel the fabric
fold onto her body warm.

She walks into a night
so close, heaven can be reached
by taking one deep breath.
Her eyes struggle to take
in beauty so extravagant.

She feels the rise
and fall of her garments
and begins to take the first
steps of dreamers dancing
under quilted nights of sequined stars.

She contemplates firework astronomy;
and makes for the road
of those who find their way.

She does not need to ask permission.

## The Remembrance of Paint

The pages have long been
At rest between folders in drawers.

The watercolours parched as the Mojave.

Brushes have gathered dust
In the shadow of curtains.

The heart of the artist, asleep.

Wake up, Dear One, to colour
In the music of life around you.

The differentiation of tone in one leaf,
The feathers of that sunbird caught up in nectar.

Pay attention again to the longings.

Wake up, oh Sleeper,
Rise into the remembrance of paint.

Make all things new for your easel,
It is time to begin again.

## Artist's Manifesto

Curve your way up through the lines
Into the heartbeat of every word,
Swap out nibs.

Paint without eyes on your back
Oblivious to impact –
Show procrastination the door.

Come down to the pulse of creation
Be a sweet observer of all things, play.
Wear a palette on your sleeve;

Elucidate the matters of spirit
In the colours that are gifted to you.
Peel off the bark of your skin, moult,

Give your new skin time to grow.
Be prepared to drop old thinking:
Wear a pair of moccasins for a day

Breathe into the lungs of the other.
Allow the music out, birth it
Don't wait another minute for a midwife,

Press into the contractions of season.
Sit at the feet of the wise ones
Who took the fork in the road long ago.

Be a grace to yourself, forgive rampantly
Bear the tools of your trade
With ease.

Remember the infinite space that resides
And be open, a channel
For what passes through.

Line the soil of your heart with compost
And mulch it, sow seeds.

Carry a lamp through the corridors,
There is fire to be fed, to be stoked
For the guests.

## Connection

The prayer for this day is for connection.
To know how much you are loved
and to have no desire for riches.

To feel the pleasure of the skin you are in
and to not count your sins against yourself.

To hold no regret against others
and to live slowly in the beauty around you.

To let your loved ones love you
and to love them without strings attached.

To grow love like gardens
and share the flowers and herbs, vegetables and fruits.

To clear your home of unnecessary clutter
so that others may benefit from what you give away.

To take a risk to trust another soul
when your soul has grown tired of trusting.

To plan something new, that you have never done,
that is not unobtainable for you.

To lay down the plentiful distractions
and listen to the call of your heart

and to take a dancing step in the direction,
a small dancing step in the direction of a dream.

It is a simple thing to connect with God
with God who abides within.

## A Psalm of the Holy Graces of Life

Your ear is turned towards my voice
and deep within my inward parts,
you are listening.

Your whole intention is given
without reserve.
You have inclined yourself to
the spaces of my heart.

Your pathways are before me certain
as the moment I was born.
You have provided for the days between
my birth and death.

The evil risen up around the earth
must be told again, and we look to see it's true,
that there are more with us each time
than those that are with them.

All holy is the pearl of your words,
dripped dew from the stem of grace.
All beauty is your soul with no beginning.

You have spread yourself glory-expansive over me
and the protection of your favour
can not be removed.

All holy is your compassion
in the dirt and fallow places where we least expect to find you.
All holy is your weeping, over the losses we have faced.

No voice can match the matchless sound of yours.
All other words fall harmless to the ground.

In love I was born, in love I live, in love I will die
and wrapped in the shield of your graces, I will live again.

## The Unknown Seas of a New Year

There is a wind blowing off the sea
urging clouds across thirsty mountains.
A sail has responded internally
setting course for the unknown seas of a new year.

The goaded feet of many travellers
have found the chains, broken,
the fetters smashed.

It was enough to be reminded
of waters from within the most Beautiful Man
that may be drawn to quench all thirst.

Amidst one Son, a countless variety
of pilgrims are voyaging, many sails aloft.

Inside, the breath of the Spirit sets the course
as we stand with wind in our faces
setting our sights on what fills the horizon.

The waves may veer us to the left or the right,
but we hear a voice directing
with true compass navigation.

As the elements swirl around us on this blustery fine day,
we know with a sure anchor
that when we come into harbour tonight
the driven strife will have blown away
and we will feel filled with open spaces
waiting to be travelled.

The map is in the hands of our Captain
and his weather-worn face assures us
that this harbour under the stars
is a place for now, to call home

until tomorrow we set sail again,
and we will be carried
by the four winds of the Spirit
into whatever's ahead.

All we need do is raise anchor,
and hoist the sails.

# About the Author

Jenneth has her poetry published with Tiferet Journal and she is part of a community of writers for the Godspace blog. Her poetry has appeared in Women's Spiritual Poetry Blog and My Utmost Christian Writers. She is the author of *Catching the Light*.

Jenneth was born in Cape Town, South Africa. After completing a degree in Library and Information Studies, Jenneth moved overseas to Toronto to complete a ministry school. She stayed on there as a volunteer and this was a life changing experience. She was healed of epilepsy and felt the tangible presence of God manifest in unusual ways. The teachings on hearing God for herself and healing life's hurts opened up a whole new world. But she learned the hard way about her tendencies to attempt to save others after going through a difficult break-up and she realised the necessity to develop healthy boundaries.

Jenneth walked into a painful season of health issues, recovering from not only the trauma of an abusive relationship, but also the shock of her brother's death. With the help of her parent's support and through working for a pastoral counselor, she began to trust the process of healing. At the same time, she developed an interest in prayer and the wisdom of many different teachers from a variety of backgrounds.

In 2016, Jenneth's family went through a process of leaving the spiritual community they had been involved with for 8 years. This grieving process of loss, recovery and healing is what became the foundation for the book you hold in your hands - *The Present Moment of Happiness*. This season of letting go of long-held dreams uncovered an invitation to adventure inwardly, and discover a new purpose and willingness to dream again.

Jenneth lives in the seaside valley of Hout Bay in the Western Cape of South Africa with her husband, Karl and three daughters. She is now a writer and home-school Mom. Karl and Jenneth have a deep desire to see people work together in unity to overcome obstacles and make the changes in their communities fueled by love and to see walls between people come down.

Through her writing, Jenneth has a desire to share hope, the ability to dream again, believe in miracles, learn to love yourself unconditionally as a healing path towards loving others, embrace your own personal power, live into the fullness of your destiny, forgive well and learn to live in the present moment with a grateful spirit, as these are all areas of ongoing growth and transformation in her own life. Jenneth is a firm believer in the fact that we never arrive, but are always changing, learning and growing - even into eternity.

# acknowledgements

I would like to express my heartfelt thanks to my sister Charmian Woodhouse for proofreading my manuscript and for her wise and helpful advice.

Grateful thanks also to Christine Sine who wrote the foreward and who has been a supportive presence for my writing as the facilitator of Godspace blog.

Great thanks to Ana Lisa de Jong who wrote the introduction, a dear friend and kindred poet who always encourages me with her life-giving poetry.

I am truly thankful to my family and friends who have been there for me and who have embraced me in my journey, so that I could in turn share it with others.

Thank you to my parents, Clive and Dorothy Lindsay who have always prayed for and believed in me.

To my husband Karl and our girls, Abigail, Sophia and Joelle who have been my ongoing support and loving strength, thank you.

I thank God who is the pulse of everything for me and the happiness to be found in the present moment.

Printed in Great Britain
by Amazon

42977914R00040